FAB Facts

FAB Facts

After four years with local newspapers, Simon Archer joined Kodak Limited's public relations division where he went on to become company press officer. In 1986 he produced a Kodak book of photographs taken by TV and radio personality Dave Lee Travis.

In recent years, he has specialized in PR consultancy work in TV, radio and, specifically, exhibition design, with the international design and project management company HBM Limited.

It was a chance meeting with modelmakers Space Models Limited, builders of many of the craft featured in Gerry Anderson's series, that brought him face to face with the creator in 1990. An interview followed for *Century 21* magazine and, some months later, they met again briefly during the interval at the London premiere of the *Thunderbirds F.A.B.* stage show. It was then that Gerry asked Simon if he would be interested in writing his biography and two months later the first of many long interview sessions began.

Within a short time Simon was also researching and writing Gerry Anderson's first UK lecture series, promoting his work in *Thunderbirds The Comic* and other sister publications and touring the country researching and photographing for this book.

GERRY ANDERSON'S

FAB Facts

Behind the Scenes of TV's Famous Adventures in the 21st Century

Simon Archer

HarperCollins*Publishers*

HarperCollins*Publishers*
77–85 Fulham Palace Road,
Hammersmith, London W6 8JB

A Paperback Original 1993
1 3 5 7 9 8 6 4 2

The publishers and author would like to thank ITC
Entertainment Group Ltd and Copyright Promotions Ltd
for their kind cooperation in the production of this book

A catalogue record for this book
is available from the British Library

ISBN 0 00 638247 9

Set in Rockwell

Printed in Great Britain by Scotprint Ltd,
Musselburgh, Scotland

To everyone who worked for AP Films and the Century 21 Organisation. It was their pioneering teamwork, led by the inspiration and drive of Gerry Anderson, that produced so much lasting, quality family entertainment for millions of television viewers around the world.

Also to my family and friends for their special support and encouragement during the preparation of this book.

Contents

Gerry Anderson's television shows have moulded and fuelled the imaginations of children, and their parents, all over the world. Many of the children who were captivated by his early work are now introducing their children to the shows with a mixture of nostalgia and, crucially, an excited enthusiasm that renews and gives these television classics new life. The shows have inspired, informed and kept on growing and entertaining. From *The Adventures of Twizzle* and *Four Feather Falls* in the 1950s, through *Supercar*, *Fireball XL5*, *Stingray*, *Thunderbirds* and *Captain Scarlet* in the 1960s, to *The Protectors*, *Space: 1999* and *UFO* in the 1970s and on to *Terrahawks* in the 1980s, Gerry's creations read like a roll call of a Golden Age of British television production. Programmed as popular audience-winning shows, they have become cult classics. And reruns worldwide are still proving that they get the ratings.

For Gerry, the future is always just beginning. His latest series is in production and will air in the UK before being screened internationally. Hard on its heels comes a slate of new television shows from his production company Gerry Anderson Productions (GAP). Gerry is now producing for the next generation. The last generation can come along too, they know they will enjoy the ride.

Adam J. Shaw
Chief Executive GAP

Foreword

'What does FAB mean?' If I had received £1 each time I was asked that question, I could have financed *Jurassic Park*. In the 1960s the buzz word was FABULOUS and it wasn't long before this was shortened to Fab, so FAB was used in *Thunderbirds* as the futuristic equivalent for 'Roger', i.e. 'Message received and understood'.

The book is based on meticulous research by the author, Simon Archer, including tapping into forty hours of interviews with me done for my biography. He also travelled the length and breadth of the country talking to many of the key technicians who worked on my shows: puppeteers, special effects technicians, model makers, voice artistes, wardrobe ladies, cameramen, directors and scriptwriters. He has taken some seven hundred original photographs from which eighty have been selected and are published exclusively in this book for the first time. As a result, it contains the most detailed photographic record on all aspects of Supermarionation puppet- and model-making ever.

When my series were first made, all the processes were a closely guarded secret, but now – after some thirty years – all is revealed. You may be surprised to know that *I* have learned one or two things about the past through reading this book! Of course, I was in charge of production, but there were some two hundred and fifty people involved and there was no way I could be everywhere at once. Nevertheless, I have carefully checked the contents with Simon and I am satisfied they *are* factual.

FAB Facts should make first-generation readers smile, perhaps revisiting their childhood, and judging from the letters I receive from the new generation of viewers, which are full of questions about the various series, it will also appeal to the whole family. *FAB Facts* is a book you can pick up and put down at any time, read anywhere and share with family and friends. Like the series, it's good, clean fun. I hope you enjoy the first 500 facts – there are many more to follow.

This is an ideal opportunity for me to thank all those who have contributed to my productions over the years. Their skill and dedication have made the shows part of British TV history. My thanks also to my wife Mary who works tirelessly with me on past and future productions, Simon Archer for undertaking this gargantuan task and, of course, HarperCollins for their enthusiasm and support.

In my view, *FAB Facts* is FAB – and that's another fact!

Gerry Anderson
London, August 1993

Acknowledgements

The author would like to thank the following people for their assistance in producing this book:

Gerry and Mary Anderson, Nick Austin (Vivid Imaginations), Steve Begg, Bob and Betty Bell, Chris Bentley, Jill and Martin Bishop, John Blundall, Mary Bridgman, Ian Boyce, John and Wanda Brown, Matthew Brown (Matchbox), Toby Chamberlain, Debbie Collings (HarperCollins*Publishers*), Barry Davies, Arthur Evans (Space Models), Alan Fennell, Dave and Liz Finchett, Cathy Ford, Ian Fryer, Christine Glanville, Richard Gregory, John Gore, David Graham, Lindsay Harris, Mark Harris, Reg Hill, Jerry Higgins (Weetabix), Peter Holmes, Val Hudson (HarperCollins*Publishers*), Bill James, Peter Joiner, Greg Martin, Derek Meddings, Bob Monkhouse, Peter Nelson, Harry Oakes, Mark Ormiston, Alan Pattillo, Brian Pugsley (Space Models), Phil Rae, Mike Reccia, Zena Relph, Roger Rice, Jo Ridgeway (HarperCollins*Publishers*), Derek Ridley (Space Models), Iris Ritchens, Desmond Saunders, Malcolm Saunders, Paddy Seale, Mark Sherwood (Moving Picture Company), Phillip Schofield, Una Scott, Adam Shaw (Gerry Anderson Productions), Lynn Simpson, Victoria Singer (HarperCollins*Publishers*), Mike Spender (HarperCollins*Publishers*), Bob Stuart (Kodak), John and Jean Taylor, Ralph Titterton, Dave Lee and Marianne Travis, Mary Turner, Karen Whitlock (HarperCollins*Publishers*), Mark Woollard.

FAB First Screenings

1957	**The Adventures of Twizzle**
1959	**Torchy the Battery Boy**
1960	**Four Feather Falls**
1961	**Supercar** (set in 1960)
1962	**Fireball XL5** (set in 2063)
1964	**Stingray** (set in 2065)
1965	**Thunderbirds** (set in 2026, although the adventures in the comic *TV21* were set in 2065)
1966	**Thunderbirds Are Go!**
1967	**Captain Scarlet and the Mysterons** (set in 2068)
1968	**Thunderbird 6**
1968	**Joe 90** (set in 2013)
1969	**The Secret Service**
1969	**Doppelgänger** (aka **Journey to the Far Side of the Sun**)
1970	**UFO** (set in 1980)
1972	**The Protectors**
1975	**Space: 1999**
1983	**Terrahawks** (set in 2020)
1987	**Dick Spanner P.I.**
1994	**G.F.I.**

FAB Facts

The term Supermarionation is derived from three words, Super, Marionette and Animation.

≷

In 1983, Supermacromation, puppetery without strings, was used in *Terrahawks*. This term comes from the words Super, Macro and Animation.

≷

The famous folding palm trees lining Thunderbird 2's runway on Tracy Island were made from paper, light cardboard and wood.

≷

In the late 1950s the very first Gerry Anderson puppet films – *The Adventures of Twizzle* and *Torchy the Battery Boy* – were shot in the small ballroom of a large mansion house, Islet Park, on the banks of the River Thames at Maidenhead.

≷

The Tracy family in *Thunderbirds* was inspired by the leading characters in the hit 1960s Western series *Bonanza* and Jeff Tracy was modelled on actor Lorne Greene.

≷

Tests for automatic movement of the puppets' mouths were first staged during the making of *Torchy the Battery Boy*.

≷

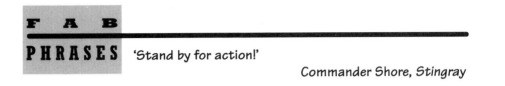

The early puppets were made from a form of plastic wood. The ingredients were powder glue, plain flour, methylated spirits, cork dust and water.

❯

Actor David Graham voiced Brains, Parker and Gordon Tracy in *Thunderbirds*. He was also one of the first people to 'voice' *Dr Who's* Daleks.

❯

A flaw in the storyline left Lady Penelope without a car or yacht by the end of the *Thunderbirds* adventures. Her Rolls-Royce FAB 1 was on board the airship Skyship One in the film *Thunderbird 6* when the craft plummeted to the ground at the end of the story. Worse still, the luxury yacht FAB 2 was sold off by her chauffeur Parker to cover his gambling debts in the episode 'Man From MI5'.

❯

Fireball XL5 was the first British children's television series to conquer the American market, being networked by NBC in 1962.

❯

Oink, the pet seal that travelled with the Stingray crew, was dropped from the series after only a few episodes.

❯

One of the world's leading pop video directors, Steve Barron, directed the 1991 Dire Straits video 'Calling Elvis', which had a strong *Thunderbirds* theme directed by Gerry Anderson.

Only a handful of the model road vehicles used in *Thunderbirds* remain in existence today.

❧

When the launch sequence of Thunderbird 2 was shot, pilot Virgil Tracy was shown being taken to the craft in civilian clothing. When the completed sequence was cut together, he was seen to have mysteriously gained a uniform. To provide continuity, a scene was later shot and added showing his uniform appearing in the cockpit.

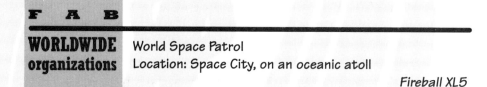

F A B

WORLDWIDE organizations   World Space Patrol
Location: Space City, on an oceanic atoll

Fireball XL5

Recently discovered – the original puppet heads of Jeff, Scott, Virgil and Gordon Tracy, together with the Hood's half-brother Kyrano and Cliff Richard Junior.

In 1967, the Century 21 Organisation had a total of seven film crews each working on its own stage.

≷

Thunderbird 5 space monitor John Tracy rarely appeared in the storylines for one reason – Gerry Anderson didn't like the character! As far as he was concerned, once John had taken the emergency call, that was that, and he remained banished to the space station.

≷

The *Thunderbirds Are Go!* feature film premiered at the London Pavilion, Leicester Square, in December 1966, where traffic was brought to a standstill.

≷

Squawks made by Mitch the Monkey in *Supercar* and Zoony the Lazoon in *Fireball XL5* were not made by animals but by a human being. Actor David Graham paid a special visit to London Zoo prior to the recording sessions to study the noises made by the monkeys!

≷

Composer Barry Gray included a new song in each episode of the puppet Western *Four Feather Falls*.

≷

The puppets' plastic hands were lined with strong wire in order to enable them to grip objects.

≷

Each episode of *Thunderbirds* cost £22,000 to produce in 1964. Today it would cost around £500,000 to make a single episode to the same standard.

≷

Tracy Island, 2.44 metres (8 feet) in diameter and carved from polystyrene (*above*).

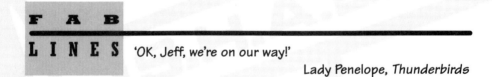

F A B

L I N E S *'OK, Jeff, we're on our way!'*

Lady Penelope, *Thunderbirds*

National Petrol sponsored a Supercar Car Club for young viewers in the early 1960s.

↯

Television Today reported in August 1962 that *Fireball XL5*'s co-star Venus provided 'all the vital, interspace glam' for the series.

↯

Henry Ford was shown the film *Thunderbirds Are Go!* and was reported to have 'loved it!'

↯

Six sculptors and two prop-makers made the original puppets for *Thunderbirds*.

❧

Three thicknesses of puppet control wires were introduced for the *Captain Scarlet* series. The strongest wires controlled the heads and bodies, finer ones moved the eyes and the thinnest of them all operated the hands. The puppet wires were 2.59 metres (8 feet 6 inches) long.

❧

Over 400,000 models of Supercar were sold in the early 1960s.

F A B

FUTURISMS   Jetmobile

Fireball XL5

A transparent plastic cup was used to make the head of *Fireball XL5*'s Robert the Robot.

❧

The larger models of the Eagle spacecraft in *Space: 1999* had working spring-loaded legs and simulated gas jet engines.

The average height of a *Thunderbirds* puppet was 56 cm (22 inches), one-third life-size.

꒰

A 'Supercar Twist' dance record was launched to coincide with the series.

꒰

On average, four and a half minutes of each fifty-five-minute *Thunderbirds* episode were shot per day.

꒰

The 2-metre (7-foot) -long version of Lady Penelope's Rolls-Royce FAB 1 cost nearly £2,000 to build (£60,000 by today's prices). Two other models of the car were used, one 46 cm (18 inches) in length and another only 7.6 cm (3 inches) long.

꒰

James Bond's faithful Miss Moneypenny was played by Lois Maxwell who voiced the character of Atlanta in *Stingray*.

꒰

During the publicity shoot for the *Thunderbirds* episode 'Attack of the Alligators', in which live creatures were used, one of the studio guests clamped its razor-sharp teeth around one of Lady Penelope's limbs. The alligator refused to let go and swallowed the leg complete with pink sandal!

'Are you going to tie me up? ... Oh, I don't mind, really.'
Lady Penelope, *Thunderbirds*

Thunderbird 4's pilot Gordon Tracy (*left*) was named after the sixth American astronaut in space, Gordon Cooper, who also journeyed on man's first day-long trip into space.

❖

The puppet bodies used in *Thunderbirds* were made from a form of porous plastic that eventually crumbled from heat and old age.

❖

Each *Thunderbirds* puppet had, on average, seven wires.

❖

In order to hide the wires from the viewers, each of them was painstakingly painted to match the colour of the respective backdrop as seen through the camera eye-piece and then, where necessary, was sprayed to prevent additional flare.

❖

In 1966, *Thunderbirds* had its own cartoon strip in the *Daily Mail*.

❖

The stun guns featured in *Space: 1999* were carved from wood.

❖

The Supercar Club had 70,000 members in 1962.

❖

Human hands were used to show close-ups of puppets picking up small objects.

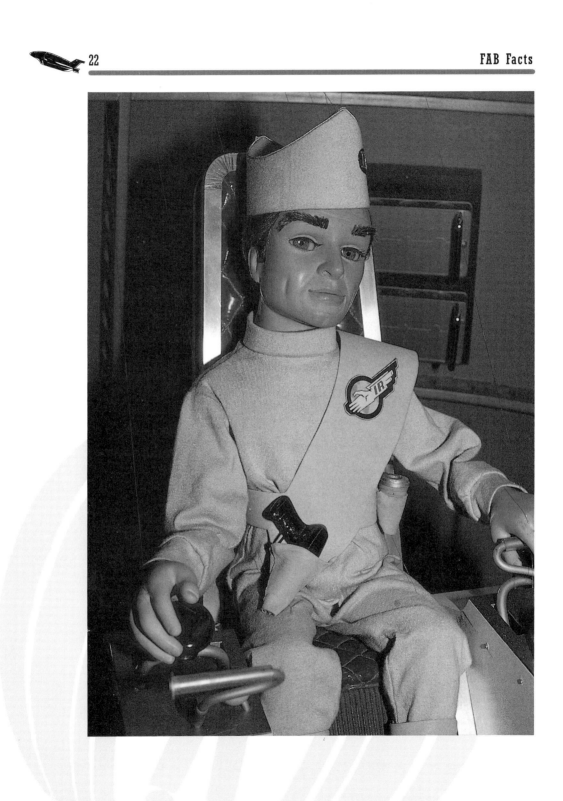

F A B

WORLDWIDE organizations

WASP – World Aquanaut Security Patrol
Location: Marineville, West Coast of America

Stingray

❧

The miniature vehicles used in the puppet shows were either pulled along the road sets by a fine wire or, in the case of the electronically driven models, steered by operators. Another method was to keep the models stationary while moving the road and background scenery on rollers.

❧

The headquarters of Spectrum, Cloudbase, in the *Captain Scarlet* series was held in 'midair' by a hidden steel rod projecting through the sky background.

❧

The studios at Islet Park became cut off by road for several weeks in the early 1960s when the River Thames burst its banks and a punt had to be used to reach the premises.

❧

The puppet face of Scott Tracy (*left*) was modelled on 1960s heart-throb Sean Connery.

❧

While in London on his 1992 Dangerous World Tour, Michael Jackson was reported to have purchased the complete set of sixteen *Thunderbirds* videos to watch in his hotel room between shows.

❧

The song played over the closing credits of *Fireball XL5*, 'I Wish I Was a Spaceman' by Don Spencer, entered the pop charts in 1963.

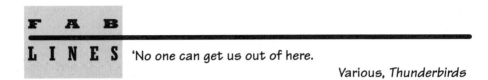

'No one can get us out of here.

Various, *Thunderbirds*

'PWOR', the response given by *Stingray*'s Troy Tempest and Phones to orders given by Commander Sam Shore, stands for 'Proceeding With Orders Received'.

❧

Fireball XL5's name was inspired by the motor oil Castrol XL.

❧

In order to keep the fish active in the underwater scenes in *Stingray*, they were fed a sprinkling of food just before filming began.

❧

Each of the puppets had miniature teeth supplied by a dental technician in Maidenhead.

❧

The puppets' eyes were made by a specialist called William Shakespeare.

❧

Mohair was used for the male puppets' hair.

❧

TV game show host Bob Monkhouse provided the voice of Brad Newman, a member of the Zero X crew, in the first *Thunderbirds* feature film *Thunderbirds Are Go!*

❧

Most of the switches on the many control consoles that appeared on the puppet shows were purchased from a second-hand radio shop in London's Lyle Street. Seen here is Jeff Tracy's TV set being remade in 1991 for the Dire Straits pop video.

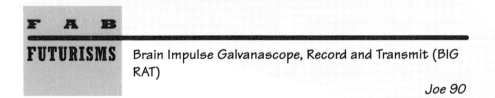

FAB
FUTURISMS   Brain Impulse Galvanascope, Record and Transmit (BIG RAT)

Joe 90

Gerry Anderson voiced only one character in all his series – Robert the Robot in *Fireball XL5*.

More than 1,500 egg boxes were used to acoustically treat the studios of AP Films in Slough where *Supercar* and *Fireball XL5* were made for the production of a commercial. An additional problem was that the premises were not soundproof as they were close to the busy A4 trunk road, the main London to Bristol railway line and also beneath the Heathrow Airport flight path.

≀

Gerry Anderson's youngest son Jamie is an avid *Dr Who* fan.

≀

If a rocket as powerful as Thunderbird 1 were to be launched through a swimming pool, as in the series, the pool would vaporize, destroying it completely, along with the nearby Tracy house.

≀

A special limited edition of *Captain Scarlet* pink champagne was produced for the launch of the series in 1967.

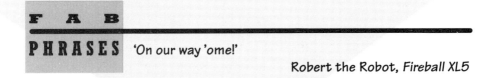

F A B PHRASES

'On our way 'ome!'

Robert the Robot, Fireball XL5

Models of *Fireball XL5* ranged in size from 12.7 cm (5 inches) to 2.74 metres (9 feet) in length.

≀

Altogether, more than 250 people worked on the making of *Thunderbirds*.

≀

Stingray was the first British TV series to be filmed in colour.

≀

To shoot scenes with puppets minus their headgear, the hats were simply slid up the wires, out of camera shot (*left*).

෫

The best place to pick up all the gossip at the studios was the unusual setting of the puppet gantry high above the studio floor. Conversations often took place on the floor below without the participants realizing that their every word was being overheard by the puppeteers above!

෫

'Making *Supercar* is very much like directing human actors, except that the puppets can't answer back!'

Gerry Anderson, 1961

෫

To make the models 'fly', the handlers would move along the gantry above the set in a smooth ballet-like fashion in order to give the craft on the end of the wires a smooth flight.

෫

The full-size version of FAB 1, built for publicity purposes only, is 6.7 metres (22 feet) long and 2.44 metres (8 feet) wide and cost the equivalent of £300,000 by today's prices to build.

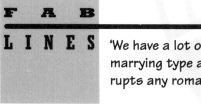

F A B

L I N E S 'We have a lot of fun together, but I don't think Troy's the marrying type and anyway, the call of duty usually interrupts any romantic notions I may have.'

Atlanta Shore, *Stingray*

At the end of each series, the studios had enough furniture and props to furnish a miniature streetful of houses.

❧

In the feature film *Thunderbirds Are Go!*, the model of the star craft Zero X cost £2,500 to build (£75,000 by today's prices) and was over 2 metres (7 feet) long.

❧

Special effects work demands a large amount of light. In the puppet studios it was particularly hot work. With the lamps and floodlights full on, temperatures often reached a blistering 49 degrees C (120 degrees F).

❧

More than 85,000 fans went to see the stars from Gerry Anderson's shows at an exhibition held in Wolverhampton in 1992.

❧

Thunderbird 5 space monitor John Tracy's face (*right*) was thought to have been modelled on actor Charlton Heston, although some say there is a resemblance with both Anthony Perkins and 1960s pop star Adam Faith...

❧

The full-size versions of FAB 1 and the Batmobile have something in common – they are both exactly the same size.

❧

The futuristic television watches worn by the *Thunderbirds* heroes were not as small as they appeared. To produce the effect, a real television image was back projected on to a small screen set into an enlarged model of a human wrist.

❧

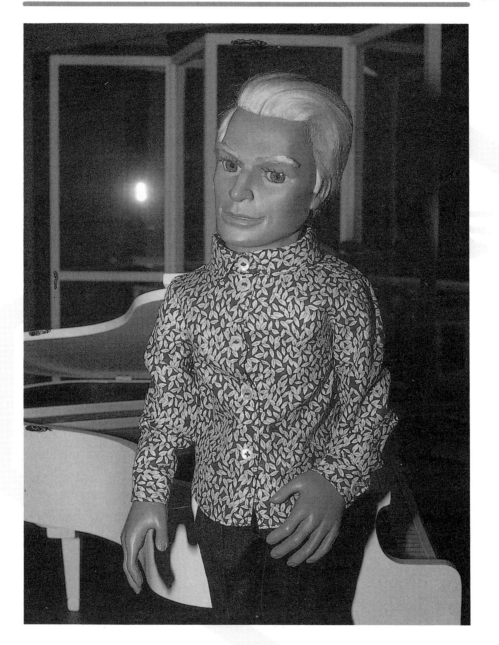

The spectacular crash scene involving the Zero X craft at the end of the *Thunderbirds Are Go!* feature film was one of the most complex scenes recorded by the puppet pioneers. It took many weeks to build the craft and only two days to destroy it!

Thunderbird 3 astronaut Alan Tracy's face was modelled on American actor Robert Reed, who at the time was appearing alongside E.G. Marshall in the lawyer and son courtroom drama series *The Defenders*.

ξ

The Mars Exploration Vehicle (MEV) was one of the few star vehicles that appeared in two different Gerry Anderson series – *Thunderbirds* and *Captain Scarlet and the Mysterons*.

FAB FUTURISMS   Hyperspace Video Phone

TV21

The Angel aircraft from the *Captain Scarlet* series was designed on a plane flight between London and New York.

ξ

For the *Captain Scarlet* series, the puppet heads were reduced in size to scale with the bodies. This was possible as the mouth movement mechanisms were no longer in the heads, but the puppets' chests.

ξ

Ed Bishop, who played Commander Ed Straker in *UFO* and voiced Captain Blue in the *Captain Scarlet* series, appeared in many other TV shows including *The Saint*.

ξ

Thunderbirds' star Lady Penelope was the world's first puppet to have a couturier.

ξ

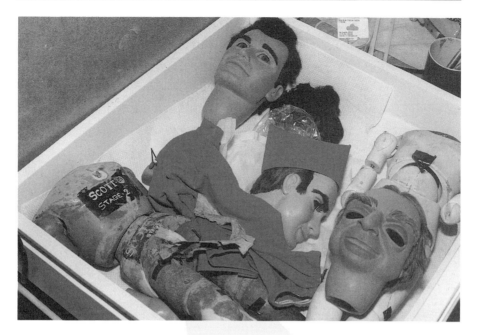

The puppet head of Troy Tempest, centre top, was rediscovered nearly thirty years after the series was made.

❯

In the early shows, *Fireball XL5* and *Supercar*, components from fireworks were used by the special effects team to create the effect of rocket motors firing.

❯

Empty cigar tubes were often raided from Gerry Anderson's office at the studios and adapted to form sections of some of the miniature spaceships' engines.

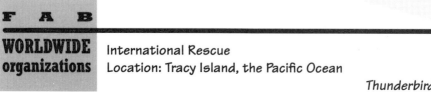

F A B

WORLDWIDE organizations

International Rescue
Location: Tracy Island, the Pacific Ocean

Thunderbirds

It was once said that enough lighting was used on the puppet shows to illuminate a small community of houses.

꛳

The collapsing palm trees lining Thunderbird 2's runway on Tracy Island were made to fall back by pulling two levers connected to two broomsticks at the end of the set.

꛳

The 'Thunderbirds March', the show's theme music, was adopted by the Band of the Royal Marines and has since been played at events all over the world as part of their official repertoire.

꛳

A large number of the models used in the shows were either destroyed during shooting or thrown away afterwards.

꛳

Thunderbirds was initially screened in sixty-six countries.

꛳

The designs for the two Rolls-Royce star cars in *Thunderbirds* and *Terrahawks*, FAB 1 and Hudson, each had to be approved by the car company before being built.

꛳

Few puppets kept their own pair of hands as most of them were interchangeable.

꛳

Gerry Anderson's first live action production, a feature film entitled *Doppelgänger*, was renamed *Journey to the Far Side of the Sun* for the American cinema audience.

꛳

Thunderbird 2 featured in every episode of *Thunderbirds*.

The first stage in making a Supermarionation puppet head is to sculpt the basic head from clay or plasticine. The finished head is made of fibreglass.

Simple ball pen lines are drawn on the exterior of Thunderbird 4 to simulate the panelling (*left*).

A tiny model of Gordon Tracy is carefully painted before being positioned at the controls of Thunderbird 4 (*below*).

One of Britain's most popular comics in the 1960s was Gerry Anderson's *TV Century 21*, which, together with its sister publication *Lady Penelope*, sold 1.25 million copies a week, a record that remains unbroken. A third comic, *Joe 90*, was also published, but only ran for thirty-four issues before merging with the more popular *TV21*.

Lieutenant Green, from *Captain Scarlet and the Mysterons*, was the only leading male black character to appear in any of the Supermarionation series.

The original launch bay for Thunderbird 1 was made largely from wood and decorated with parts from model kits bought from a toy shop near the studios.

The puppet heads in *Terrahawks* were made from rubber, allowing greater expression in the characters' faces.

Generally, the puppets did not have feet. Their feet and shoes were made as one and attached directly to their legs.

The appearance of
Stingray's Troy Tempest
was based on American
film star James Garner.

Dental acrylic was used for
making the puppet eyes, the
same material that goes into the
making of false eyes for humans.

FAB 1's headlights were made
from battery-powered bicycle
lamps.

Parker's voice was modelled on a
waiter at the King's Arms,
Cookham, who used to work at
Windsor Castle for "Er Majesty".

After a long break from British TV
screens, *Captain Scarlet and the
Mysterons* returned in 1993, supported by another massive
merchandising campaign. Here
we see some of the products from
the 1960s and the 1990s.

The face of *Stingray*'s evil sealord Titan was modelled on Sir Laurence Olivier.

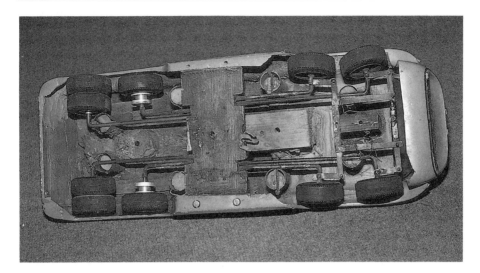

Most of the miniature road vehicles in the puppet series had independent suspension as in the case of this one (*above*) that appeared in both *Thunderbirds* and *Captain Scarlet and the Mysterons*.

❯

Toothpaste tube tops were used as dials on many control consules in the early shows.

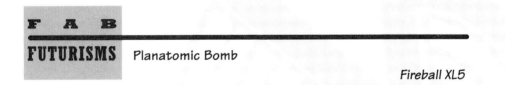

F A B

FUTURISMS   Planatomic Bomb

Fireball XL5

Operating the puppets in the *Captain Scarlet*, *Joe 90* and *Secret Service* series was not easy, largely because the heads were reduced in size to scale with their bodies, and became too light to move with ease.

❯

From *Thunderbirds* onwards, several puppets, including the Hood, were operated from underneath in some scenes.

Remote-controlled model aircraft were used in the second *Thunderbirds* feature film, *Thunderbird 6*.

᠈

Gerry Anderson's navy blue Rolls-Royce appeared in the opening titles of the 1973 series *The Protectors*, starring Robert Vaughn and Nyree Dawn Porter.

᠈

Composer Barry Gray added an extra dimension to the puppet shows through his music and unique futuristic sound effects.

᠈

The *Captain Scarlet* series had its own pop group – The Spectrum.

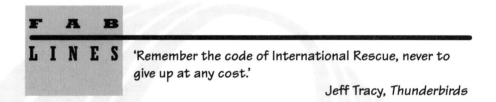

F A B

L I N E S   'Remember the code of International Rescue, never to give up at any cost.'

Jeff Tracy, *Thunderbirds*

Initial inspiration for the face of the Lady Penelope puppet came from a photograph of a model in a shampoo advert found in a copy of the glossy fashion magazine *Vogue*.

᠈

Gerry Anderson's favourite road vehicle from his many series is the Shadomobile in *UFO*.

᠈

Alka Seltzer tablets were used to create the water bubbles in some underwater scenes and also to simulate fat frying in a pan.

᠈

In the 1960s, each puppet was valued at about £250. Today, the surviving original puppets, such as Colonel White (*above*), are each worth thousands of pounds .

Thunderbird 2 frequently returned to the special effects workshops for repair when the wires suspending the craft snapped. These wires carried the power to fire the rockets, four underneath and two in its tail. If too much power was supplied, the wires would quickly become red hot, glow and break.

Glycerine was carefully dropped on the cheeks of the puppets' faces to simulate tears.

Much of the 1993 reconstruction work of the Supermarionation puppets took place in a small shed nestling in the shadow of the 007 stage at Pinewood Studios, Buckinghamshire.

In the *Thunderbirds* episode 'Terror in New York City', Thunderbird 2 was attacked and crash-landed on Tracy Island. For this scene, a large model of the famous craft was destroyed during filming. The special effects team carefully chose one particular model for this purpose that was not perfect in detail!

FAB FUTURISMS   Light Refraction Video Corrector

TV21

The prestige car manufacturer Rolls-Royce stipulated that Lady Penelope's car, FAB 1, was always referred to in full – as 'the Rolls-Royce' – disallowing any reference to 'the Rolls' or 'the Roller'.

A puppeteer has much more control over his or her puppet when it is controlled from underneath rather than by strings.

Some of Lady Penelope's fab fashionwear is still in existence today.

≷

FAB 1 was designed with six wheels not just because it had to carry a large and powerful engine, but simply to make it look different from any other car.

≷

Few scenes in *Thunderbirds* date the show, but there is one in particular where Lady Penelope is a) Smoking b) Not wearing a safety belt and c) Wearing a mink coat!

≷

To achieve greater realism with miniature cars, the special effects team would place a thin layer of dust on the model roadway. This was then disturbed by tiny jets fitted to the underside of the cars.

≷

The first puppet head of *Stingray*'s Titan was dropped on the work-shop floor and smashed to pieces minutes after it was completed.

❧

The rocket lift-off scene in the film *Doppelgänger* was filmed outdoors using models against the backdrop of the natural sky. The set was located in the studio car park.

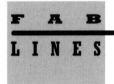

FAB LINES

'If we don't help, the entire world could be destroyed.'
'That's quite a statement.'

John and Jeff Tracy, *Thunderbirds*

To simulate perspiration on the puppets' faces, an ordinary tooth-brush was soaked in water and the bristles flicked to spray tiny droplets on to the small faces.

❧

Each episode of *Captain Scarlet and the Mysterons* was originally planned to include a star guest voice and puppet to match. The idea never took off, but, in the pilot episode, the puppet of the World President was modelled on actor Patrick McGoohan.

❧

A selection of puppets were known as 'revamps', the name given to the guest artist puppets which, apart from their eyes, were faceless. Temporary faces were sculpted using plasticine for individual episodes.

❧

When aerial shots were required, the solution was to remove the raised rostrums and locate the sets on the studio floor.

❧

The model of the futuristic Rolls-Royce Hudson, the star car in *Terrahawks*, was made from this prototype carved from solid wood (*above*).

ξ

The WASP fighter aircraft in *Stingray* were constructed from a series of ordinary plastic model kits, with their wings modified.

ξ

To make the evil Hood in *Thunderbirds* more powerful in appearance than his co-stars, he was given a larger head and bigger, stronger-looking hands.

ξ

Some of the trickiest models to suspend from wires were the alien craft in *UFO*.

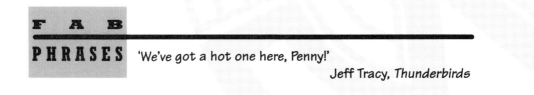

F A B

PHRASES   'We've got a hot one here, Penny!'

Jeff Tracy, *Thunderbirds*

In one scene in the first episode of *Captain Scarlet*, a camera followed a car down a spiralling road leading down from a high storey car park tower. Instead of the camera following the car, it remained static and the entire set was rotated.

≷

At least one major scene containing an explosion was filmed each working day during the making of *Thunderbirds*.

≷

While 'flying' the model craft on wires over a set, the special effects technicians at the controls would often be heard making simulated jet noises not unlike children at play!

≷

Pirate radio in the 1960s, in the form of Radio Caroline, inspired Gerry Anderson to include a pirate radio station in space in one episode of *Thunderbirds*.

≷

Originally, according to aficionados, an alternative theme tune was considered for *Thunderbirds*. Following on the style of earlier shows, a song was recorded entitled 'Flying High'. Although never used as a theme tune, the song was featured in the episode 'Ricochet'.

≷

The coloured sashes on the International Rescue uniforms were made of a stiff fabric, buckram, before being covered in leather.

≷

The image of *Stingray*'s Agent X20 was based on actor Claude Rains.

≷

Real trees – juniper – were used to add realism to the outdoor scenes.

≷

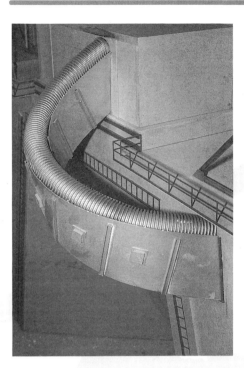

A domestic vacuum cleaner pipe was used to make the launch tube of Thunderbird 2 (*left*).

꒕

The top 1960s ITV game show *The Golden Shot*, hosted by Bob Monkhouse, was given a *Captain Scarlet* theme for one programme.

꒕

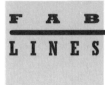

F A B

L I N E S 'I wish I had a little boy of my own that would help me. Oh, I've a wonderfuful idea. I'll make a toy-boy.'
Mr Bumbledrop, *Torchy the Battery Boy*

Lady Penelope was always dressed in the best miniature clothes, many of which were made from real furs including mink, coney and leather.

꒕

Special effects director Derek Meddings succeeded in staging his own personal vertical takeoff out of the studio water tank when he realized that a live alligator, appearing in the *Thunderbirds* episode 'Attack of the Alligators', was on the loose!

꒕

Positioning the puppets on the sets prior to filming was a time-consuming and exacting process.

❧

Over 200 versions of the Thunderbird crafts were constructed, from entire models down to specific sections for close-up filming.

❧

In 1966, Gerry Anderson received two accolades for his work on *Thunderbirds*. He was awarded the silver medal for Outstanding Artistic Achievement by the Royal Television Society and was made an Honorary Fellow of the British Kinematograph Sound and Television Society.

❧

Cold coffee was poured on to the costume of the nasty Zelda in *Terrahawks* to make it look old.

❧

The designers of Concorde claimed to be avid fans of *Thunderbirds* when it was first screened. When Concorde was rolled out at Toulouse in France, it was greeted by the Band of the Royal Marines playing the 'Thunderbirds March'.

❧

The theme song for *The Protectors*, 'Avenues and Alleyways', sung by Tony Christie, entered the Top Forty in 1973.

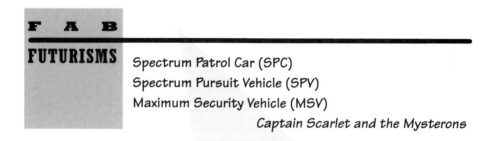

F A B

FUTURISMS   Spectrum Patrol Car (SPC)
Spectrum Pursuit Vehicle (SPV)
Maximum Security Vehicle (MSV)
Captain Scarlet and the Mysterons

The *Sunday Mirror* newspaper once described Lady Penelope as 'an advertisement for British fashion'.

❧

One particular episode of *Space: 1999* was entitled 'The Rules of Luton'. American scriptwriter Freddie Freiberger, who also worked on the early series of *Star Trek*, was inspired by a signpost at junction 11 on the M1 motorway!

❧

Actor Francis Matthews based the voice of Captain Scarlet on movie star Cary Grant.

❧

Radio and TV game show host Nicholas Parsons voiced the leading character of Tex Tucker in *Four Feather Falls*.

❧

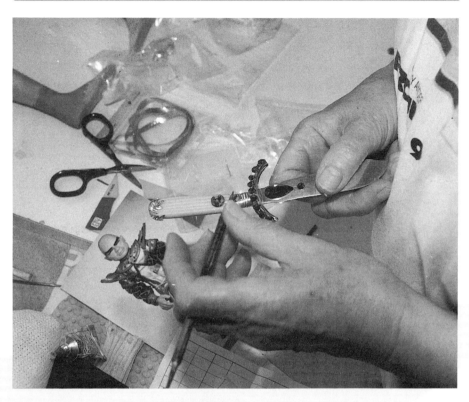

The Hood's sabre was made from an old butter knife (*above*).

❧

The then newly constructed and unopened M40 motorway in Buckinghamshire was used for some daredevil flying scenes in the feature film *Thunderbird 6*.

❧

The underwater shots in *Stingray* were recorded using an aquarium measuring 2.44 metres by 1.22 metres (8 feet by 4 feet) and made of 1.3 cm (1/2-inch) plate glass. The model craft didn't enter the water, but was flown on wires behind the 9,000-litre (2,000-gallon) tank.

❧

Production came to an abrupt halt on the 1969 live-action series *UFO* when leading actor Ed Bishop broke his ankle during filming.

The puppets' beds were made with specially hollowed-out mattresses in order to give the effect of weight from the puppet.

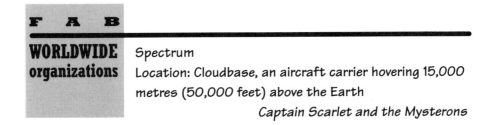

F A B

WORLDWIDE organizations

Spectrum
Location: Cloudbase, an aircraft carrier hovering 15,000 metres (50,000 feet) above the Earth
Captain Scarlet and the Mysterons

One of Lady Penelope's two mink coats took a week to make and was given the fashionable title of 'Miss Minx'.

One of Gerry Anderson's initial brief for the comic *TV21* was that it should be 'different from anything that had been done before'.

The sound of boiling porridge, slowed down, was used to simulate that of molten lava.

HRH the Princess Royal was introduced to Lady Penelope at the Royal Windsor Rose Show in 1992. She was reported to have glanced down at the puppet and commented 'Oh no! How horrible!'

One of the most difficult puppets to operate was Robert the Robot in *Fireball XL5*. He lacked weight and balance.

Strange things used to happen to the *Thunderbirds* puppets on some occasions when the studios were closed at night. Lady Penelope was often found next morning in a compromising position with one of her colleagues...

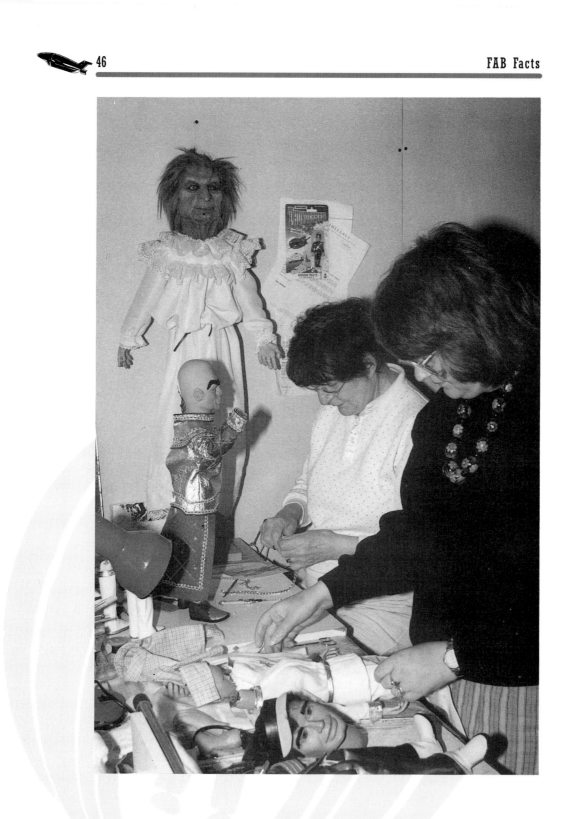

It took, on average, eleven hours to make a single puppet costume (*left*).

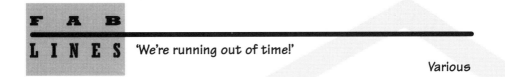

'We're running out of time!'

Various

Up to five sample versions of the face for the blonde puppet Venus from *Fireball XL5* were made before one finally received approval. The winning head was based on the appearance of Sylvia Anderson.

Star of stage and small screen, Phillip Schofield has been a fan of *Thunderbirds* since an early age and has unhappy memories of the time his younger brother Tim buried his die-cast model of Thunderbird 2 in their family back garden.

Actor Windsor Davies, star of BBC TV's *It Ain't Half Hot Mum*, voiced the Zeroid robot Sergeant Major Zero in *Terrahawks*.

Lavatory blocks were adapted to form space-age headphones worn by Nicholas Parsons and Denise Bryer in a TV commercial directed by Gerry Anderson in 1960.

The puppet face of Mrs Appleby in *The Secret Service* was modelled on the mother of chief puppeteer Christine Glanville.

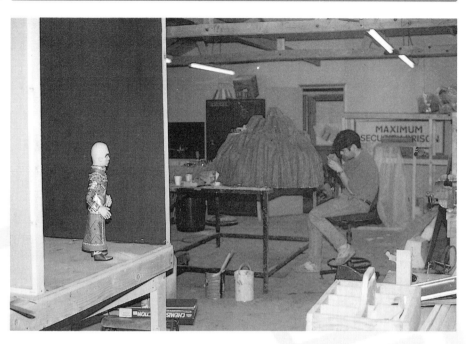

The biggest-ever model of Tracy Island (*above*) was built in 1993 for the '*Thunderbirds* and the World of Gerry Anderson' exhibition in Blackpool.

➤

Ordinary nail varnish was used to give a shine to the puppets' shoes.

➤

The larger sets used in the early Anderson puppet shows had to be designed to incorporate two large pillars that supported the ceiling of the ballroom studio at the mansion house in Maidenhead.

F A B

FUTURISMS Sting Missile

Stingray

The cockpit of Thunderbird 1 was rebuilt for a TV commercial in 1992. The craft's air grill was made from a soap dish, empty hand-cream tubs formed parts of control panels and a hairspray can was disguised to look exactly like a fire extinguisher.

❧

Thunderbirds The Comic editor Alan Fennell was one of the main script writers for *Fireball XL5*, *Stingray* and *Thunderbirds*. He was also the first editor of Gerry Anderson's hit 1960s comic *TV21*.

❧

The star car in *UFO* was later owned by TV and radio personality Dave Lee Travis.

❧

Thunderbird 5 space monitor John Tracy was originally going to be cast as one of the leading Tracy sons piloting one of the rescue craft.

❧

TV's most famous spook family, the Munsters, were a popular feature in the *TV21* comic.

❧

Thunderbird 3 astronaut Alan Tracy was named after Alan Shepherd, the first American astronaut in space.

❧

Thunderbirds began as a series of half-hour shows and the first nine episodes had to be extended when the order was given to lengthen each episode to one hour.

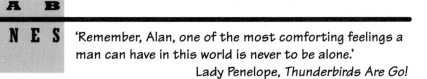

F A B

L I N E S   'Remember, Alan, one of the most comforting feelings a man can have in this world is never to be alone.'
Lady Penelope, *Thunderbirds Are Go!*

When the initial concept for *Thunderbirds* was drawn up, it was agreed that Kyrano's daughter Tin Tin should have a 'romantic interest' in Thunderbird 3 astronaut Alan Tracy (*left*).

Thunderbirds art director Bob Bell was arrested while cutting tree clippings in Burnham Beeches, Buckinghamshire, to dress a set.

The Daleks, minus Dr Who, appeared in the early issues of the *TV21* comic.

Chunks of coal from a local coal-yard in Slough were painted grey and used on the sets to simulate rocky landscapes.

Each craft was lined with asbestos in an attempt to prevent them from catching fire when the 'engines' were ignited.

The fish that appeared to swim around the Stingray craft were between 1.3 cm (half an inch) and over 7 cm (3 inches) in length, to give the illusion of both depth and scale.

The salmon-like leap of Stingray and a Titan Terror Fish in the opening titles of the series was achieved on the first take.

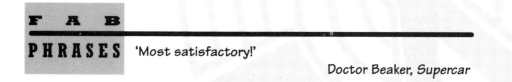

F A B

PHRASES 'Most satisfactory!'

Doctor Beaker, *Supercar*

Many of the jet engine noises made by the Thunderbird craft were recorded at Little Rissington Airfield, Gloucester.

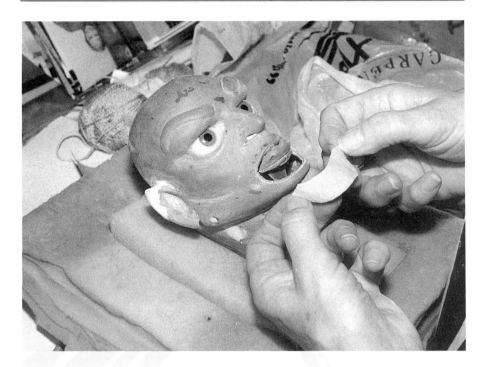

Condoms were used in tests to find a suitable material to cover the area below the moveable lower lip of the early puppets. In the end, good quality fine leather provided the solution (*above*).

⊰

Children's BBC TV star Edd the Duck had to go one better than the *Blue Peter* programme in the 1993 rush to 'build-your-own' Tracy Island. The star duck appeared on TV with his own Sharon Island.

⊰

The first special effects sequence to be produced by the TV puppet pioneers was the rocket launch in the opening titles of *Torchy the Battery Boy*, ably assisted by some firework sparklers.

⊰

A number of episodes of *Thunderbirds* were edited down and dubbed into French and also Hindi for schools programmes in 1992. 'Thunderbirds Chelga!' is Hindi for 'Thunderbirds Are Go!' A year later, episodes from the same series were dubbed into Gaelic.

≷

Puppets became even more detailed for the second *Thunderbirds* feature film *Thunderbird 6* and in one sequence a puppet actually showed the fillings in his teeth when he laughed.

≷

Thunderbird 2 is Gerry Anderson's favourite aircraft from the fifteen TV series he has produced.

≷

Puppet dresser Zena Relph made 209 costumes for the characters that appeared in *Terrahawks*.

F A B FUTURISMS World Videophone

Stingray

One of the most intricate special effects shots to be made at the Slough studios was for the feature film *Thunderbird 6* where Thunderbirds 1, 2 and 6 and FAB 1 travel for some distance in convoy across a specially made set running the length of the studio floor.

≷

The first Troy Tempest puppet that appeared in the early episodes of *Stingray* in 1964 had a squint.

≷

The *Thunderbirds* episode 'The Perils of Penelope' was a take-off of the silent movie *The Perils of Pauline* starring Pearl White.

The miniature chairs were given low seats to allow for a more natural-looking posture from the puppets (*left*).

❭

Real human eyes were photographed and used to form the puppets' eyes in the *Captain Scarlet* series.

❭

Flexible puppet bodies were introduced for the *Joe 90* series to allow the characters to be positioned with their arms and/or legs crossed.

❭

Tin Tin's name comes from the Malaysian word for 'sweet'.

❭

The HQ interior set used in *Supercar* was redressed and used to form the control room at Space City in *Fireball XL5*.

F A B
WORLDWIDE organizations

WIN – World Intelligence Network
Location: London, England

Joe 90

The large rocket model featured in the film *Doppelgänger* was badly damaged in an accidental blaze at the studios shortly before filming began.

❭

A full-size multicoloured striped Mini, containing two large pandas, featured in Gerry Anderson's comic photo strip series 'Candy and Andy'.

❭

Gerry Anderson's pet Great Dane, Penny, was featured in one episode of *The Secret Service*. The large dog was filmed chasing a puppet across a lawn. In order to attract Penny, the puppet was painted with aniseed.

❯

The pilot episode of *The Investigator* (1973) was made using puppets and remote-controlled models and shot entirely on location in Malta.

❯

The Mysterons, 'Sworn Enemies of Earth' in the *Captain Scarlet* series, were regularly featured in two comics in 1967, *TV Tornado* and *Solo*.

❯

Part of the reason for the great popularity of *Thunderbirds* today is because interest in the series has spanned several generations, as its creator Gerry Anderson is constantly reminded (*below*).

Two different waistlines were introduced for the *Thunderbirds* puppet bodies. Scott and John Tracy appeared thinner than their brothers, giving the illusion that they were taller with broader shoulders. In fact, they were all the same height.

❧

Operating puppets with 'strings' created a challenge when it came to passing through doorways on the sets. A film trick was used to overcome this. The character would be filmed approaching the door which was shown complete with frame. At the same time, the camera would zoom in on the puppet, excluding the top of the door. With the camera still rolling, the top section of the door was then removed. The puppet, still in close-up, would then appear to walk smoothly under this apparent section.

F A B

FUTURISMS   Surface Video Scan

Stingray

The Angel aircraft that appeared in *Captain Scarlet and the Mysterons* were made in two sizes – 18 cm (7 inches) long and 46 cm (18 inches) long.

❧

The pink clouds used in the dream sequence in the *Thunderbirds Are Go!* feature film were made artificially by dropping dry ice (frozen carbon dioxide) into buckets of water.

❧

The puppet heads contained solenoids that moved the mouths in synchronization with a pre-recorded voice-tape.

❧

A different technique was used to show spacecraft in flight in the series *Space: 1999*. Instead of the craft being 'flown' on wires towards the camera as, say, with Thunderbird 2 in *Thunderbirds*, the Eagle craft was supported by a steel rod fixed to a black wall and, rather than the Eagle moving towards the camera, the camera would move towards the model.

❧

A specially devised technique, named the roller road, was introduced at the studios to show the effect of vehicles moving along a road. The models were kept stationary while the road and separate background and foreground scenes moved by on rollers at differing speeds to give the impression of perspective. First used in the pilot episode of *Thunderbirds*, this technique went on to be used throughout the film industry.

❧

Captain Scarlet's illuminated epaulettes were made of brass and nylon.

❧

The aluminium futuristic cars used in *UFO* were not particularly roadworthy and were rarely used on public roads.

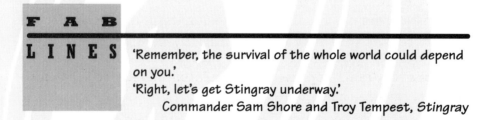

F A B

L I N E S

'Remember, the survival of the whole world could depend on you.'
'Right, let's get Stingray underway.'
Commander Sam Shore and Troy Tempest, *Stingray*

The strange lumpy eyebrows belonging to Maya (Catherine Schell) in *Space: 1999* were made from plastic mounted on adhesive tape.

For the film *Thunderbirds Are Go!*, three factory warehouses housed up to five sets at a time for shooting different scenes.

❧

The first model of Thunderbird 2 was carved in a fine grain jelutong wood and from this moulds were taken and cast in fibreglass. Using this process, the model was kept in good shape and was both lightweight and rigid.

❧

To achieve the spacewalks in *Space: 1999*, the actors were suspended from the roof of the studio and shot using high-speed cameras to make their movements appear more graceful.

❧

For the making of the *Thunderbirds* TV series, there were two puppet units, each with three puppeteers.

❧

The moving colours shown behind Commander Straker's desk in *UFO* were created by simply projecting a rotating slide on to a white Perspex panel.

F A B

FUTURISMS Ski-thrusters

Thunderbirds

The model craft that appeared in *Thunderbirds* weighed anything from 113 g (4 oz) to 9 kg (20 lb).

❧

Lady Penelope was the first to utter the phrase 'F.A.B.'

❧

Real seashells decorated the set of Titan's throne room in *Stingray*
(*above*).

❯

Seajet, Zoom, FAB and Orbit were all names given to ice lollies that
were linked with the puppet heroes in the 1960s.

❯

Howard's Way star Tony Anholt appeared in Gerry Anderson's *The
Protectors*.

❯

In the early 1980s, then Capital Radio DJ Mike Smith began a
campaign to bring *Thunderbirds* back to British television screens.

❯

Three-dimensional sets were introduced with *Torchy the Battery Boy*.

❯

Model Penny Snow toured Britain during the summer of 1968 dressed as a Lady Penelope lookalike to publicize the *Thunderbird 6* film.

F A B

L I N E S   'He's really minty.'

Tin Tin, *Thunderbirds*

Former *Mission Impossible* stars Martin Landau and Barbara Bain set up home in England while *Space: 1999* was in production.

❖

During discussions in the early 1980s to bring a new series of *Thunderbirds* to our screens, there were plans to do away with Lady Penelope's Rolls-Royce, FAB 1, and provide her with a Porsche.

❖

Gerry Anderson's first job was as a passport photographer.

❖

During the filming of *The Adventures of Twizzle*, a new device known as video assist was invented that is now in use in film-making worldwide. It involves placing a TV camera to the eye-piece of the camera to provide a picture, normally only seen by the camera operator, to everyone on the studio floor and particularly the puppeteers.

❖

Carry On film star Kenneth Connor voiced the characters of Rocky, Dusty and Pedro in *Four Feather Falls*.

❖

A fishing line was used to pull Supercar out of the water and into flight as can be seen clearly in the show's opening titles.

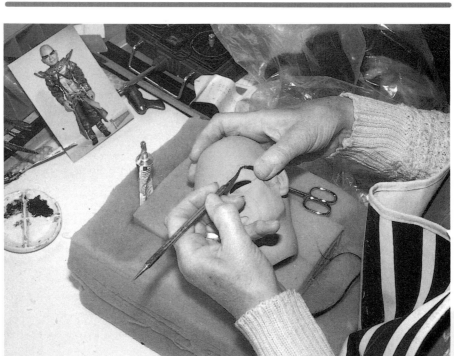

A careful process of cutting and glueing is used to apply the famous large eyebrows to the Hood puppet (*above*).

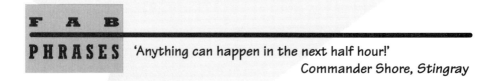

PHRASES   'Anything can happen in the next half hour!'
                                          Commander Shore, *Stingray*

Actor Stanley Unwin, master of 'Unwinese', otherwise known as 'gobbledegook' language, twinned with a puppet lookalike to co-star in *The Secret Service*.

❧

Actor Shane Rimmer voiced the popular character of Scott Tracy in *Thunderbirds* and more than twenty years later returned to play the lead in the pilot show for Gerry Anderson's latest concept *Space Police*. He also wrote several scripts for *Joe 90* and *The Protectors*.

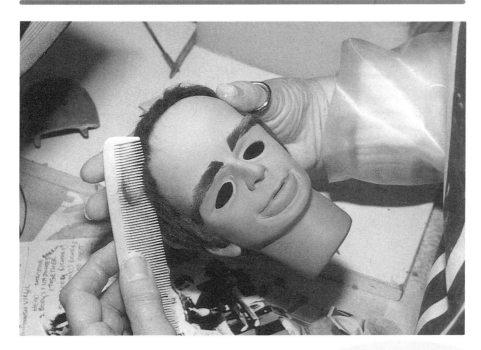

Applying hair to a puppet's head is a slow process, finished off by a trim and a comb (*above*).

≷

Thunderbirds was the first series from the West to be shown in colour on Japanese TV screens.

≷

The *Thunderbirds* special effects unit produced up to eighteen shots a day and often worked late into the night.

≷

More than half a million people of all ages have seen the *Thunderbirds* stage mime show at home and abroad.

≷

A space costume used in the *Space: 1999* series cost £600 at the time to produce.

In an attempt to get *Thunderbirds* back into production in 1983 Gerry Anderson created a new format. He had plans to shed Brains's bespectacled, stuttering 1960s image. The Brains of the 1980s was going to become a clear-sighted, eloquent young man, keen on home computers.

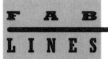

'International Rescue hasn't heard the last of me!'
The Hood, *Thunderbirds*

Denise Bryer, voice artist for the nasty Zelda in *Terrahawks*, also voiced the character of Noddy for an early radio series.

❧

Parents queued outside toy shops through the night during the build up to Christmas 1992 in order to be first through the doors to grab the few *Thunderbirds* toys available.

❧

Gerry Anderson produced his first pop video in 1983. *Terrahawks*'s puppet character Kate Kestrel had a real-life double, 19-year-old student Moya Griffiths, who performed 'SOS Mr Tracy'.

❧

Each pair of feet/shoes had the character's name written on them during the first stage of production *(see page 65)*.

❧

Channel 4 star Dick Spanner's character was based on a combination of film detectives Philip Marlowe and Inspector Clouseau.

❧

Brains's famous spectacles were made from a piece of blue plastic found lying around the studio. The hinges came from a real pair of glasses purchased from the Slough branch of Woolworths at a cost of two and a half pence.

The original models of the Titan Terror Fish craft from *Stingray* were made using cardboard for their bodies and wood for their heads. More recent models have been made of a type of resin.

When not in front of the
cameras, the Lady
Penelope puppet wears
her own hairnet.

At least three sizes of
Thunderbird 3 were built
for the TV series, the
largest being over 1.8
metres (6 feet) tall. Nearly
thirty years on, a similarly
detailed smaller model
has been produced.

Once painted, the models of the Thunderbird craft were dirtied down to add further realism. This was an important element in making many of the shots appear totally believable, and it is a recognized modelling technique in use today.

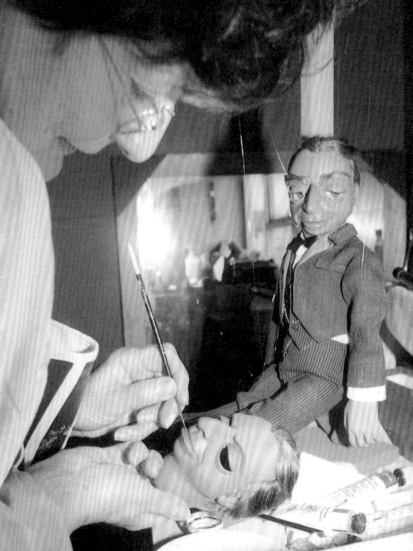

One of the original Parker puppets was used to match a head for a new duplicate puppet.

Several of the original puppet bodies are still in use today.

One of the reptilian aquaphibian creatures in *Stingray* made a debut appearance in the earlier series *Fireball XL5* under a slightly different guise.

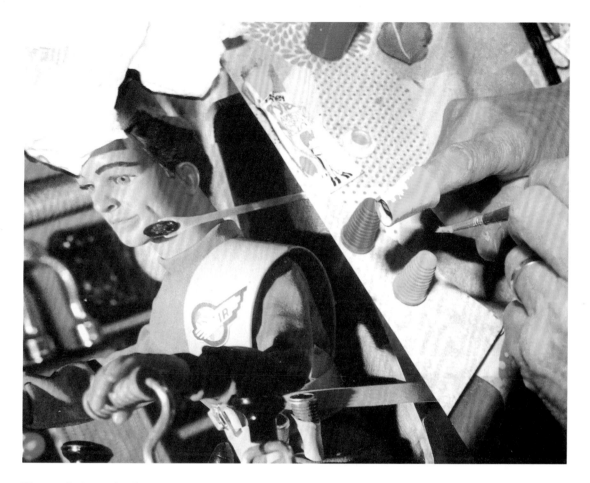

The gun holsters for the Thunderbird pilots are carefully cut from small pieces of leather before being painted to match the respective pilot's uniform.

More than two million die-cast models of FAB 1 were produced at the Dinky Toys factory in Liverpool when *Thunderbirds* first appeared on television.

Puppet buckle belts are made from the straps on toy watches.

In all, 20 million die-cast Dinky Toys were made in the 1960s relating to Gerry Anderson's series. Some of them are shown here together with their present-day Matchbox counterparts.

An exact miniature replica of one of the shirts belonging to lead singer Mark Knopfler was specially made for his puppet double's appearance in the Dire Straits video for their 1991 single 'Calling Elvis'.

Thunderbirds art director Bob Bell does a spot of vacuuming on the set of the Tracy lounge, rebuilt in 1991 for a brief appearance in the Dire Straits pop video.

The zip on Captain Scarlet's uniform is adapted from a tank track taken from a model kit.

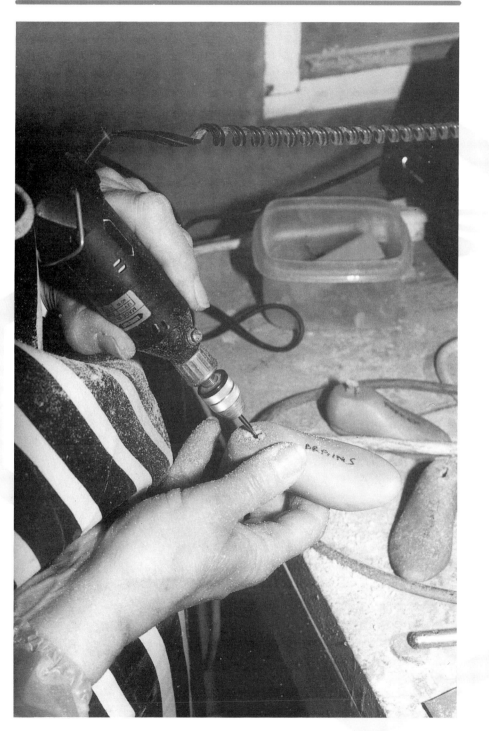

Fanderson, the official Gerry Anderson appreciation society, was launched in 1981. It has more than 2,000 members worldwide, and is one of the largest TV-related fan clubs in the UK.

FAB

FUTURISMS Clearvu

Supercar

The set of Marineville in *Stingray* was made out of cardboard for lightness.

❧

The *Thunderbirds* phrase F.A.B. is simply a shortened version of the word 'fabulous' which was the in-word in the 1960s.

❧

The voice of Titan's sidekick, Agent X20, in *Stingray* was modelled on the voice of actor Peter Lorre.

❧

A continuity error occurred during Tracy Island's 'operation cover-up' at the end of the first episode of *Thunderbirds*. In one shot, the portrait pictures of the Tracy boys in casual gear mysteriously reverted to the more official pictures of them in uniform, which could have blown their cover completely to the island's guest who was standing nearby.

❧

The first Supermarionation series *Four Feather Falls* was also featured in the children's comic *TV Comic*, alongside Popeye, Mighty Moth and Beetle Bailey.

❧

Comedians Peter Cook and Dudley Moore staged a TV spoof of *Thunderbirds* in the 1960s, renaming the show *Superthunderstingcar*.

F A B

WORLDWIDE organizations

BISHOP – British Intelligence Service Headquarters
Operation Priest
Location: Central London, England

The Secret Service

There are between 90 and 130 special effects in each episode of Thunderbirds.

Today, reproduction puppets made to stand without strings have foam bodies lined with wire (*below*).

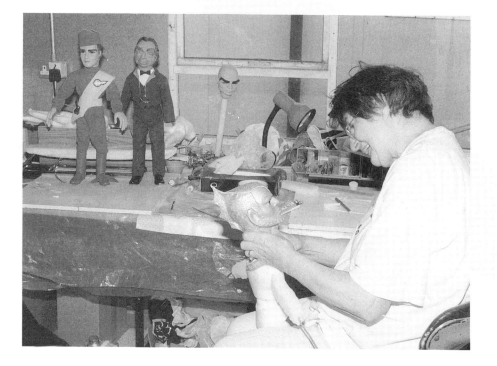

Pop legend Dave Stewart recorded the theme music for Gerry Anderson's first animated series *GFI*.

Fans screamed with delight at the sight of puppet guest star Cliff Richard Junior at the London premiere of *Thunderbirds Are Go!*

With the *Thunderbirds* revival in the early 1990s came speculation from the fashion press that 'perhaps one of the most influential names for Spring 1992 is not Jean Paul from Paris, or Giorgio from Milan, but Gerry from Kilburn', as fashion trends mirrored the 1960s puppets' gear.

The first water tank used on the set of *Stingray* for the underwater scenes burst, flooding the studio.

A complete three-dimensional miniature Western street set was built for the cowboy puppet series *Four Feather Falls*.

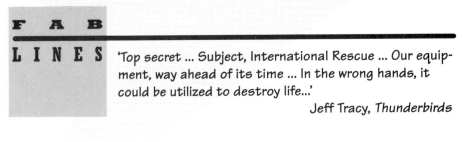

FAB LINES

'Top secret ... Subject, International Rescue ... Our equipment, way ahead of its time ... In the wrong hands, it could be utilized to destroy life...'

Jeff Tracy, *Thunderbirds*

Gerry Anderson's first TV puppet series *The Adventures of Twizzle* was made on a tiny budget of £250 per fifteen-minute episode.

Composer and musician Barry Gray created unique sounds and atmospheric music for the *Fireball XL5* series.

As with the big screen movies, a traditional clapperboard is used for each scene (*above*).

≷

The Dinky Toys die-cast model of Captain Scarlet's SPV, Spectrum Pursuit Vehicle, was the manufacturer's highest selling product ever.

≷

In 1973, Gerry Anderson produced a one-off educational film, entitled *The Day After Tomorrow – Into Infinity*, that focused on Albert Einstein's Theory of Relativity.

≷

The Stingray craft was given its name before it was even designed.

≷

The Thunderbird craft were originally going to be named Rescue 1, 2, 3, 4 and 5.

≷

An average day's shooting of the early puppet shows began at 8 a.m. and went through to 1 a.m. the following morning.

'Well, Brains, your phenomenal mind made all this possible. Now, you're going to see it in action.'

Jeff Tracy, *Thunderbirds*

Mickey Mouse was Gerry Anderson's favourite cartoon character when he was a child.

≀

Despite the vast number of hazard-ridden storylines in *Thunderbirds*, few of the characters were ever killed off.

≀

Four film stages were used initially for the shooting of *Thunderbirds* – two for puppetry and two for special effects.

≀

Bridge-building kits for model railways were bought up in large volume to provide the components for larger suspension bridges on the sets.

≀

Thunderbirds had one major advantage over its predecessors: it was an hour in length, thereby allowing for greater story development and characterization.

≀

Many of the puppets' characters evolved as each series progressed in production. Lady Penelope and Parker began as secondary characters in *Thunderbirds* and went on to become two of the most popular in the series.

Craftsman Bill James, the man who built some of the first models for *Supercar*, *Fireball XL5*, *Stingray*, *Thunderbirds* and more, returned to the workshop to reconstruct the cockpit of Thunderbird 2 in 1993 (*above*).

 Autobomb Detonator Unit

Thunderbirds

The Slough factory units that once formed the film studios of AP Films and later Century 21 Productions now house a plastics manufacturing company.

During the making of *Thunderbird 6*, a special twenty-four-hour workshop was set up in the special effects unit that specifically dealt with repairs to the radio-controlled model craft that had 'crash-landed' during filming.

Stingray's rotating power unit at the rear of the craft frequently broke down on the special effects film set.

≷

Each *Thunderbirds* puppet consisted of at least thirty components.

≷

The idea for the movement of Titan's Terror Fish in *Stingray* was inspired by the traditional twisting fairground snake-on-a-stick toy.

≷

The panel lines on the Thunderbird craft were drawn in using an ordinary 2B pencil and then smudged for effect.

≷

From high up on the puppet gantry, chief puppeteer Christine Glanville watches the scene below on a TV monitor (*right*).

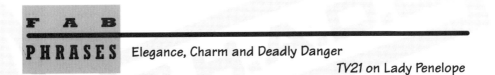

PHRASES   Elegance, Charm and Deadly Danger

TV21 on Lady Penelope

The scene where an elevator car crashes out of control as the Fireflash airliner attempts an emergency landing in the first episode of *Thunderbirds* was not in the script. The shot was an out-take where the model concerned careered off the set accidently. It looked so good they decided to use it after all.

≷

Thunderbird 2's wings were swept forward simply to be different from conventional aircraft design.

≷

Although there was only one person operating each puppet, the puppet bridge over the set often became very congested during the shooting of crowd scenes.

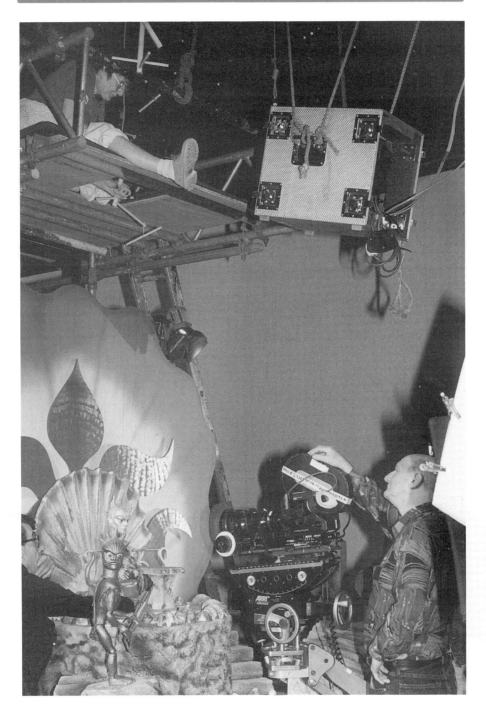

To add to the timeless quality of the *Thunderbirds* series, great attention was paid to the smallest detail. For example, none of the cars had registration plates giving away the date.

❧

Frustrated with the difficulties over trying to make the puppets walk, Gerry Anderson decided to turn to science fiction in 1961 and to place the characters in vehicles to bypass the problem. The first of these was Supercar. The characters in *Fireball XL5* were provided with jetmobiles.

❧

Inspiration for the *Thunderbirds* episode 'Attack of the Alligators' came from the H.G.Wells book *Food of the Gods* and the Bob Hope film *The Cat and the Canary*.

F A B

FUTURISMS   *Phonovision*

Thunderbirds

In one *Stingray* story, a small island was blown up. The minor explosion caused a mini tidal wave in the water tank, resulting in the cameraman getting a soaking.

❧

Stingray was made in colour for the American audience, but then transferred into black and white for most of the remaining TV audiences around the world who were still viewing in black and white at the time.

❧

One half-hour episode usually consisted of an average of 250 individual scenes.

The edges are smoothed off on a new model of the super sub Stingray (*above*).

In one of the 1960s publicity photographs of Parker, he is holding a silver tray with a letter on it addressed to 'Agent X20, Island of Lemoy'. Agent X20 was not in *Thunderbirds*, but the earlier series *Stingray*.

From 1964, finished film left the Slough studios at the rate of half an hour a week.

Each of the three stages at the Slough studio measured 12 metres by 14 metres (40 feet by 45 feet) – tiny by ordinary film standards.

Voice artists often played up to four characters from any one series.

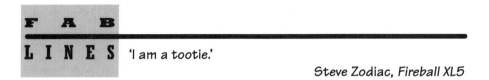

F A B
L I N E S 'I am a tootie.'

Steve Zodiac, Fireball XL5

Making a puppet dance is not easy. In the *Thunderbirds* episode 'The Cham Cham', Lady Penelope was seen performing a slow foxtrot, with one puppeteer controlling her strings from above and another holding on to her feet out of camera shot.

Back projection played an important part in the successful production of both *Supercar* and *Fireball XL5*.

All the parts that go into making Thunderbird 3 are laid out ready for the assembling process to begin (*right*).

The *Thunderbirds* series was originally going to be entitled *International Rescue*.

Steve Zodiac from *Fireball XL5* appeared in TV commercials for the Lyons Maid Zoom ice lolly. While the series was filmed in black and white, this commercial was made in colour for the cinema audience.

One of the most complex puppet scenes to film was the journey Virgil Tracy took from the Tracy lounge to his craft Thunderbird 2, via the flip-over wall picture and a series of sliding shoots.

Filming some of the special effects scenes for *Thunderbirds* demanded that the film crew wore protective clothing, including safety helmets and gas masks.

F A B

FUTURISMS   Astrascope

Fireball XL5

Sawdust, sand, fuller's earth and gravel were used to decorate the exterior sets.

❧

The voice of the duchess in the *Thunderbirds* episode 'The Duchess Assignment' was provided by Australian actor Ray Barrett, who also voiced the Hood.

❧

When the model of Thunderbird 2's main fuselage was lifted on to its telescopic legs, leaving its pod on the ground, the structure sometimes weakened, resulting in the front section of the craft breaking away.

❧

Perhaps the most ingenious feature of Thunderbird 5 was an electronic interpreter that translated all languages immediately into English.

❧

At the beginning of the *Thunderbird* series, Thunderbird 2 was the only craft to be armed, as it was perceived as being less manoeuvrable and more vulnerable to attack.

F A B

PHRASES   *'Well done, boys!'*

Jeff Tracy, Thunderbirds

Century 21 Records produced some of the UK's first stories on disc in 1964 (*above*). Thirty-seven were recorded in total, each taking the form of a mini album containing '21 Minutes of Adventure'.

❧

By 1966, *Stingray* had netted £3 million in programme sales to independent TV stations around the world.

❧

Special long-duration charges were developed by a rocket propulsion company to simulate the Thunderbird craft's engines firing.

❧

Century 21 was one of the names first considered for the spaceship Fireball XL5.

❧

Each Supermarionation puppet had only four teeth – those that were visible to the camera.

≷

The budget for the *Thunderbirds Are Go!* feature film was £250,000 in 1966.

≷

Two huge water tanks were used for ocean effects. Water was continually pumped in and, like a weir, poured out at the far end, giving a lifelike horizon line.

FAB FUTURISMS   Thruster Pack

Fireball XL5

By the mid 1960s, Gerry Anderson had been labelled 'the Walt Disney of this millionaire micro-miniature world'.

≷

Some of the model cars contained a device for dipping the bonnet when the vehicles came to a halt.

≷

The average *Thunderbirds* puppet weighed about 4 kg (8 or 9 lb).

≷

In one episode of *Captain Scarlet and the Mysterons*, 'The Inquisition', Captain Blue is seen to fall from a window on board the airborne HQ Cloudbase. Visible for a split second is a large human hand giving the puppet a shove!

≷

The Slough studios where *Stingray*, *Thunderbirds*, *Captain Scarlet and the Mysterons*, *Joe 90*, *Secret Service* and some scenes for *UFO* were shot (*above*).

⋜

To create the effect of thick black smoke for the crash scenes in *Thunderbirds*, burning rubber proved very effective.

⋜

The Secret Service was only broadcast in three ITV regions, Scottish TV, ATV and Southern TV.

F A B

WORLDWIDE organizations

SHADO – Supreme Headquarters Alien Defence Organization
Location: Beneath Harlington Straker Film Studios, near London, England

UFO

Destiny Angel, from *Captain Scarlet and the Mysterons*, was modelled on 1960s pin-up Ursula Andress.

⋜

Lumps of glass specially sought from local glass furnaces were used to simulate iceberg scenes.

❧

In the *Thunderbirds* episode 'City of Fire', a hefty G-clamp is seen to crash down in front of the camera in a scene where a building roof collapses.

❧

Space: 1999 was one of Britain's most expensive TV series ever made, costing £300,000 per episode at the time.

❧

One of the original models of *Stingray* was made from hollowed out balsawood.

❧

Tiny pieces of model kits provide the extra detail for communications equipment hidden away on Tracy Island (*below*).

The character of Lady Penelope was aged twenty-six in Thunderbirds.

The voice of Virgil Tracy changed during the production of *Thunderbirds* when Jeremy Wilkin took over from the original artist David Holliday.

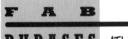

'Thunderbirds are go!'

Jeff Tracy, *Thunderbirds*

A genuine Rolls-Royce radiator was used to shoot the close-up sequence of the cannon firing from FAB 1.

Up to four puppet characters could be made to 'talk' at once using the automatic lip sync method first introduced in *Four Feather Falls*.

The puppet gantry where the puppeteers worked from was 7.6 metres (25 feet) long.

The puppet hats had fine holes drilled away to allow for the wires controlling the heads.

The legs of Thunderbird 2 were made of brass.

The Lady Penelope puppet never wore short skirts. They would have revealed the ball-and-socket joints in her knees.

≷

A prototype for a model jet aircraft with a 1.52-metre (5-foot) wingspan, capable of reaching speeds of 100 m.p.h. at heights of up to 6,000 metres (20,000 feet), was developed by AP Films in the mid 1960s. It never got off the ground.

≷

A large section of the rear of each of the Supermarionation puppet heads was detachable. Here we see inside the head of *Stingray*'s Troy Tempest.

≷

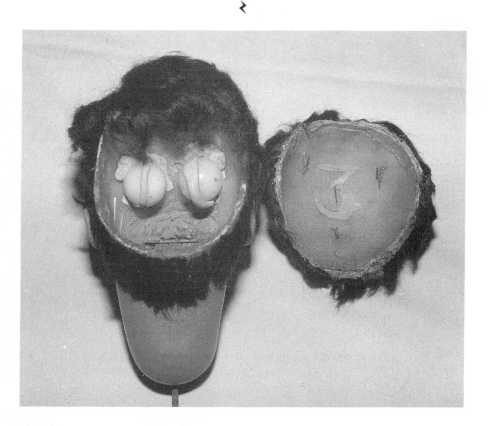

'Adults over 16 should be accompanied by children' exclaimed the advertisements for the feature film *Thunderbirds Are Go!*

F A B
WORLDWIDE organizations

Terrahawks
Location: A secret base in South America

Terrahawks

The tail wheels from a real aeroplane were used to form the undercarriage of the puppet version of the Tiger Moth Thunderbird 6, which appeared in the film of the same name.

❮

A 2-metre (7-foot) -long model of Supercar was built in 1960 at a cost of £1,000 (£40,000 by today's prices).

❮

The colour process used for the filming of *Stingray* was named Videcolor. Hudsoncolor was adopted ten years later for *Terrahawks*.

❮

The only Supermarionation series to be set in the then present day were *Supercar* (1960) and *The Secret Service* (1969).

❮

More episodes of *The Protectors* were made than any other Gerry Anderson series. There were fifty-two in all.

F A B
FUTURISMS

Automatic X-ray Camera

Thunderbirds

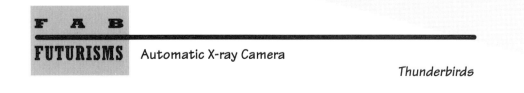

Space: 1999 was also featured in comic strip form in *Look-In*, the junior *TV Times*.

❧

The face of Melody Angel from *Captain Scarlet and the Mysterons* was thought to have been modelled on singer Eartha Kitt.

❧

During the 1960s, it was reported that more than 50 per cent of Dutch television viewers watched *Thunderbirds* every week.

❧

Each of the twenty-two episodes of *Dick Spanner P.I.* was only six minutes long.

❧

Two of the many titles considered for *Space: 1999* were *UFO: 1999* and *Space Journey: 1999*.

❧

Film star Roger Moore is thought to have once told fellow actor Francis Matthews, voice of Captain Scarlet, that he believed the puppet's face was modelled on him.

F A B

L I N E S   'I say, open this door at once, we're British!'

Sir Jeremy Hodge, *Thunderbirds*

To portray the effect of a gun firing in *Four Feather Falls*, the flash was painted on to the film negative with black ink.

❧

The creator of the Daleks, Terry Nation, was behind the idea to do away with space suits and provide the crew of *Fireball XL5* with oxygen pills while walking in space.

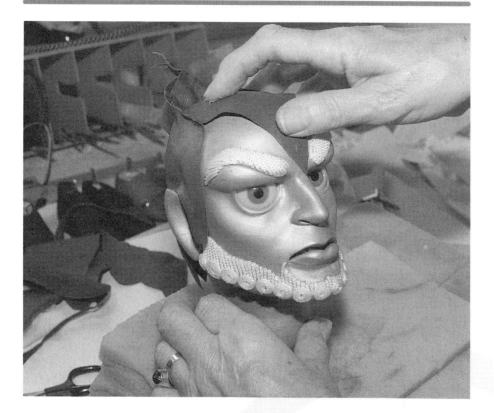

Titan's headgear takes shape, carefully cut from leather and allowing holes for the all-important strings (*above*).

❯

The small explosions staged by the special effects department were filmed at high speed so that when they were played back at normal speed the action was slower and therefore the size of the explosions appeared much larger.

❯

There were few punch-ups in the Supermarionation shows as this was a virtual impossibility in puppetry terms.

❯

The face of red-headed Rhapsody Angel, from *Captain Scarlet and the Mysterons*, was based on 1960s model Jean Shrimpton.

FAB FUTURISMS   Contra-Rotating Antistorque Eddy Damper
Stingray, TV21

The puppet shoes were made from real leather.

The wardrobe department stocked more than 700 miniature costumes at any one time during the making of *Thunderbirds*.

Space: 1999 was a reworking of a possible second series of *UFO*.

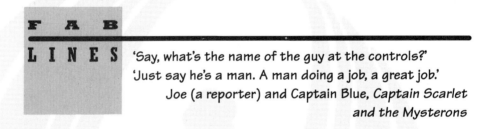

FAB LINES   'Say, what's the name of the guy at the controls?'
'Just say he's a man. A man doing a job, a great job.'
Joe (a reporter) and Captain Blue, *Captain Scarlet and the Mysterons*

'Breath-taking entertainment' is how the *News of the World* newspaper described the feature film *Thunderbirds Are Go!*

Lady Penelope's majestic home, Creighton Ward Manor, was based on Stourhead House in Wiltshire.

A national newspaper spotlighted the likeness between Prime Minister John Major and a bespectacled Joe 90.

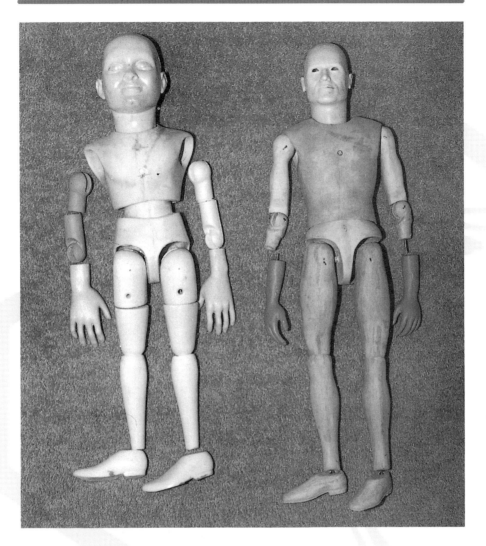

The puppets' hands and heads were reduced in size to exactly one-third life-size for the *Captain Scarlet* series (*above*).

❧

Linen carpet thread was used for suspending the early puppets.

❧

A British international rescue corps was inspired by *Thunderbirds*.

Human false eyelashes were trimmed down and used to perform the same role for the puppets (above).

⟩

Real hair was used for the puppets of the Dire Straits band.

⟩

Moonbase controller Gay Ellis, in *UFO*, was played by Gabrielle Drake who later appeared on the soap scene as owner of the famous Crossroads Motel.

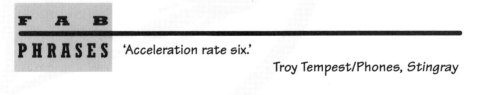

F A B

PHRASES *'Acceleration rate six.'*

Troy Tempest/Phones, Stingray

A model shot of Concorde was made for a promotional film at the Slough studios before the supersonic aircraft flew.

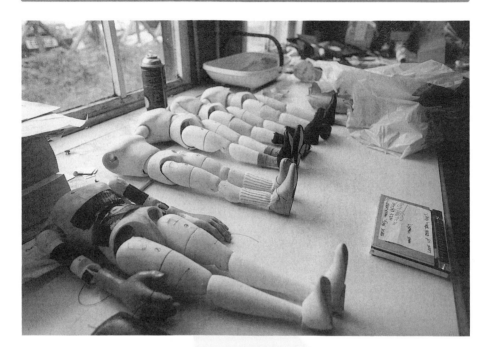

The puppet bodies of the Dire Straits band line up in the workshop in readiness for further surgery (*above*).

The driving seat of FAB 1 was positioned in the centre of the car.

In order to show a fleet of Eagle transporters in *Space: 1999*, often only one model was used. A group of shots was combined to form a composite, a technique later used by film director George Lucas in the blockbuster movie *Return of the Jedi*.

A Japanese TV company produced a cartoon adaptation of *Thunderbirds* entitled *Thunderbirds 2086*. It was not a Gerry Anderson production.

Ed Straker's car in *UFO* was built on the chassis of a Ford Zephyr.

Each of the main puppet characters had, on average, five heads –
two had normal expressions and the remainder included one
'smiler', a 'blinker', and a 'frowner'. This picture shows the original
'normal' and 'smiler' heads of Captain Blue from the *Captain Scarlet*
series.

❧

Thunderbird craft sculpted from ice decorated the London Hilton for
the reception following the premiere of *Thunderbirds Are Go!*

The title British Telecom appeared on the side of a building in *Thunderbirds* long before the organization's name was adopted officially in the UK.

≷

The appearance of Harmony Angel, from *Captain Scarlet and the Mysterons*, was modelled on actress Tsai Chinn who starred in several Hammer Horror productions.

≷

The model of the set of Moonbase in *Space: 1999* was 4.5 metres (15 feet) square.

≷

Only one complete model of Thunderbird 5 was made for the TV series.

≷

A computer-controlled tank came under fire in an episode of *The Secret Service* from an aircraft from another series. The attacker was an Angel Interceptor from *Captain Scarlet and the Mysterons*.

≷

Former *Neighbours* star Gary Files, who played Tom Ramsey in the popular Australian soap, voiced a number of characters in *Captain Scarlet*, *Joe 90* and *The Secret Service*.

≷

Brains from *Thunderbirds* was thought to have been modelled on actor Anthony Perkins.

≷

The Stingray craft made a guest appearance on the *Des O'Connor Show* in the 1960s when the super sub surfaced in the singer's bath.

FAB LINES

'Keep this frequency clear.'

Scott Tracy, Thunderbirds

FANDERSON is the official appreciation society for everyone who enjoys the work of Gerry Anderson. Full details are available by sending a stamped addressed envelope to: Fanderson, P.O. Box 93, Wakefield, West Yorkshire WF1 1XJ.

Published quarterly, *Century 21* is the official Gerry Anderson magazine for followers of his work. For subscription details, contact: Engale Marketing, 332 Lytham Road, Blackpool, Lancs FY4 1DW.

Other specialist publications monitoring closely the work of Gerry Anderson include: *TV Zone*, *Time Screen*, *Starlog*, *Starburst*, *Model and Collectors' Mart*, *Comic World*, *Comics International*, *Epi-log* and *Science Fiction Modeller* (Australia/New Zealand).